BURT FRANKLIN: BIBLIOGRAPHY & REFERENCE SERIES 301
Essays in Literature & Criticism 44

SHAKESPEARIAN PUNCTUATION

SHAKESPEARIAN PUNCTUATION

A Letter
Addressed to the Editor of "The Times."
October 26, 1911

T. J. COBDEN-SANDERSON.

BURT FRANKLIN
NEW YORK

Published by BURT FRANKLIN
235 East 44th St., New York, N.Y. 10017
Originally Published: 1912
Reprinted: 1969
Printed in the U.S.A.

Library of Congress Card Catalog No.: 73-108427
Burt Franklin: Bibliography & Reference Series 301
Essays in Literature & Criticism 44

SHAKESPEARIAN PUNCTUATION

MAY I, FROM WITHIN THE LIMITS OF my own experience, write a few lines in support of the vindication by Mr. Simpson of "Shakespearian Punctuation" & of your admirable article upon the same subject in to-day's issue? When I undertook the reprint of Shakespeare's Sonnets, thinking that for so exquisite a form of poetry the punctuation should be as exquisite, I decided to make an exception to my rule of following the text and to revise what had superficially seemed to me arbitrary and haphazard in the punctuation of the original. I accordingly revised the punctuation of the 1609 edition, sonnet by sonnet; & a fascinating & alluring balancing of nice probabilities I found it to be: but as I proceeded I found two other & more important things, first, that slowly, like the coming on of night, I was changing the whole aspect of the Sonnets, and, secondly, that the original punctuation had a method in its seeming madness, though its method was not the method of to-day; that, in fact, it was based, not on logical or grammatical structure, but on emphasis and literary gesture. I therefore cancelled all the sheets I had already printed, both vellum and paper, and began the edition over again, keeping, with few exceptions, punctiliously to the punctuation, and to all the other characteristics, of the original. ⁋ But as seen by yourself, Sir, the question raised is much larger than the vindication of the printers of the First Folio or of the Sonnets;

nor is it a question only of the appreciation of another method or system of punctuation. It is a question also of the presentment to-day of the literature of an earlier time, and I submit that the presentment to-day of the literature of an earlier time should be its re-presentment as it was under the conditions of its own time, and not as it would or should be under the conditions of to-day. And I would go the length of saying that even were the punctuation of Shakespeare not as systematic and purposeful as on the whole it would now appear to be, it yet should be preserved in any & every serious edition of his works. Old work loses incalculably in its appeal & charm when robbed of it own apparel and made gaudy in scholarship for the footlights of modern criticism. All honour to modern scholarship, but all honour also to the steps, faltering or firm, by which that scholarship has been reached. Again, all literature, both ancient and modern, has its place in history, in the retrospect of the whole life of the world, and should be thought of in time and space and appreciated in its integrity and in relation to that larger whole of life; finally, that larger whole of life is itself a tentative work of art produced in time by the general genius of mankind, operating progressively under widely different conditions, & admitting of conservation intact only by the conservation intact of all its constituent parts. ⟨ The importance of Mr. Simpson's contribution to this question lies, in my opinion, in calling attention to the integrity of literature in all its stages, and to the scholarship which consists in capacity to appreciate literature, and to respect it, in each stage of its development.

T. J. COBDEN-SANDERSON.

The Doves Press,
 October 26.